A Guide to the Design, Production, and Sale of Salary Surveys

Association Edition

TED TURNASELLA

www.wagelink.net

A Guide to the Design, Production, and Sale of Salary Surveys

Association Edition

TED TURNASELLA

www.wagelink.net

in cooperation with

DataMotion Publishing, LLC

New York

A Guide to the Design, Production, and Sale of Salary Surveys

Library of Congress Control Number: 2011939027

ISBN: 978-0-9815831-5-0

DataMotion Publishing, LLC

1019 Fort Salonga Road, Suite 10-333

Northport, NY 11768-2209

www.datamotionpublishing.com

Table of Contents

About the Author

Ted Turnasella, M.S.

Ted Turnasella develops effective compensation policies and plans that support the business objectives of his clients. There are many kinds of pay plans including base pay plans, sales incentive plans, variable pay plans, and executive compensation plans. Several principles guide the design of effective pay plans. A good pay plan will:

! Always encourage effective job behaviors and discourage ineffective job behaviors.

! Present a clear and coherent proposition to the employee.

! Represent a fair exchange of economic value.

Ted Turnasella began his career after college working as a field economist for the Bureau of Labor Statistics. The responsibilities of the job included gathering survey information on wages and benefits from companies in multiple industries. His next job was with Chase Manhattan Bank in New York City, where he worked as a job analyst for several years. Subsequently he worked for several years as a manager in the retail industry, after which he accepted a position with Avis, Inc. where he worked for three years as a job analyst. Ted was, then, offered an opportunity to build a new pay plan for a manufacturing company in Glen Cove. Some years later Ted joined Newsday as its Compensation Manager. After nine

5

years with Newsday, Ted decided to open his own compensation practice, Comp-unications, in 1995.

In 2002, Ted opened Wage*LINK*, an on-line, interactive, salary survey database. Using the Wage*LINK* technology, any group of companies can establish a salary survey group for themselves on the Internet. Participants can select the jobs they want to survey, determine the profile of their group members, and update their records in the survey database at any time and as often as they wish. To ensure high quality wage and salary reports, all records submitted to Wage*LINK* are reviewed for quality before being released to the database. Wage*LINK* received a U.S. Patent in 2007.

Mr. Turnasella has over 30 years of experience as a compensation professional both in the corporate world and as an independent consultant. His experience covers many industries including manufacturing, banking, publishing, retail, pharmaceutical, biotechnology, social services, financial services, internet, power generation, and travel. His client list includes First Data Corporation, Pall Corporation, Suffolk County National Bank, Municipal Credit Union, The Nielsen Companies, Newsday, L-3 Communications, Underwriters Laboratories, and Estee Lauder. He has published many articles for professional journals, spoken at the national conference level, and has appeared on network television as an expert speaker on compensation issues.

Mr. Turnasella holds a bachelor's degree from Saint Peter's College in Jersey City and a Masters Degree in Labor and Industrial Relations from New York Institute of Technology. He is a member of The Society for Human Resource Management, the Long Island Compensation Association, and WorldatWork.

About Wage*LINK*

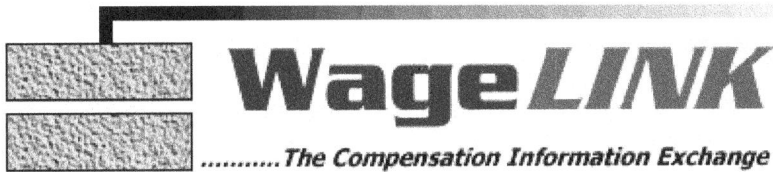

Wage*LINK*
..........The Compensation Information Exchange

Wage and Salary Surveys

Wage*LINK* is an interactive database that allows any number of companies to create their own unique salary surveys on the Internet. You already know how necessary wage and salary information is for managing a business; but, unlike most wage and salary surveys, Wage*LINK* provides you and other participants with flexibility that has never been possible before... except through very expensive custom surveys.

Wage*LINK* is designed to provide you with salary information on benchmark jobs in two ways:

First, the Wage*LINK* on-line database contains salary information on hundreds of benchmark jobs, based on records submitted by more than 300 companies.

Second, as a survey hosting service, Wage*LINK* enables any number of companies to create their own unique Salary Survey Groups. You and your peers can exchange information on benchmark jobs that are difficult (if not impossible) to find anywhere else, in a confidential, professionally-managed environment.

For more information about Wage*LINK*, just go to www.wage-link.net.

Warning–Disclaimer

While this book strives to provide the reader with practical guidance and to provide general education on the topic at hand, it is not a substitute for adequate legal or other professional advice. The opinions within represent the opinions of the authors and editors only and, therefore, should not be construed as a position on the part of any particular organization or entity.

Further, nothing herein should be construed as the rendering of legal or other professional advice and the reader is advised to consult with appropriate counsel for obtaining any advice. By reading this publication, no attorney client relationship exists between the reader and either the author or publisher.

Introduction

If your organization has decided to design, produce, and sell a salary survey, then you are, in effect, opening a new business. You will have to make the same decisions that any business person would make. Your success will depend on how well you plan out your new enterprise and the resources you have available to support your efforts.

The purpose of this guide is to help you think through the issues you will face. But it is **only** a guide. As always, a little common business sense will help you solve many of the challenges you will encounter along the way.

We have attempted to cover the production of salary surveys in the broadest application, namely producing a salary survey that may be provided at little or no cost to your association's members; and which may also be sold at a profit to non-members.

Depending on your objectives, some of the process steps described herein may not be necessary.

The sections of this guide have been arranged in the form of questions which should be answered if you are to produce a salary survey for your members or others.

Good Luck! If you have any questions, please call me at
(631) 699-0667.

Ted Turnasella
President
Wage*LINK*, LLC
ted@wagelink.net

1

Establishing Objectives

Understanding your objectives will help you make decisions all through the process of designing, producing, and distributing a salary survey. A good business plan will help you think through the steps that will need to be taken to reach your objectives.

Do we want to make a profit? If you do, how much?

One of the first decisions to face is whether you are conducting the survey to make a profit for your association; and, if so, how much of a profit would you like to make. Salary surveys can be an excellent means of adding to your organization's treasury making it possible to offer additional benefits to members. In addition, offering the survey for sale to non-members, may allow you to provide the survey to members at little or no cost.

Do we want to use the salary survey to drive up membership?

Perhaps you intend for the salary survey to promote membership in your association. You can accomplish this by differentiating the price you charge for your survey between members and non-members. Offering a substantially lower price to members will encourage non-members who wish to purchase the survey to join your association.

Will the salary survey be a means to retain members?

In addition, as with any value-added service or product, salary surveys can be a great way for your association to retain members who wish to continue to obtain the survey at little or no cost. To strengthen the retention of members, you could limit the survey's availability to members only. The downside of this strategy, of course, is that you may sell fewer surveys resulting in lower revenue and profit for your association.

What risks will we face if we proceed with our plans to produce a salary survey?

At some point you will need to think through the possible risks associated with producing a salary survey. Here are a few to consider.

There is always the unintended loss of money. Salary surveys can be costly to design and produce depending on how much work can be done by volunteers, how much data is collected, and how the survey will be distributed. These days, with email and document management software, e.g. Adobe, the costs associated with printing and distributing surveys can be minimal. If you choose to engage the services of an outside consultant to design the survey, process the data, and/or produce the final report you will probably incur a significant cost.

Another risk would be the loss of prestige for the association if the survey is not done well; which, in turn, could lead to a loss of members.

Finally, there can be some legal risk associated with conducting wage surveys.

The body of anti-trust law generally treats wages as prices. Fixing prices is illegal, as is fixing wages which would limit competition or restrain trade in the labor market. So you need to be careful that you do not violate anti-trust laws. The Department of Justice and the Federal Trade Commission have developed some safe harbor guidelines which you can follow to limit this risk. *(See Exhibit 1: Antitrust Issues)*

Here are the guidelines:

1. Use an independent third party to manage the survey to ensure that all survey data is kept confidential. Your association can act as this third party or you may choose to hire an outside consultant to fill this role.

2. Ensure that records used in the survey report are at least three months old.

3. Watch out for *dominance*, which is allowing one large payer in the survey to account for more than 25% of the data points in a weighted average for a particular job.

4. Use at least five data points to calculate survey averages and percentiles.

Note: To be safe, it would be wise to consult an attorney to make sure that your survey process will meet the legal safeguards for conducting and producing a salary survey.

What opportunities will we have if we go forward?

Along with risk there comes opportunity. Think through the opportunities that a salary survey will present to your organization. Here are a few.

Salary surveys can provide a very valuable and vital service to your members and others who want to manage the salary costs of their companies more intelligently. Your association may be able to provide those companies with data that is simply not available anywhere else at any price.

The survey data that you provide will be more credible than that contained in other published surveys because it comes from trusted members and usually represents the <u>true</u> labor market in your geographic region or industry or both.

Also, as mentioned above, salary surveys can be an excellent source of income that can subsidize or enhance other benefits or activities for members.

And finally, a survey gives you a wonderful opportunity to form alliances with other associations that can enrich and expand benefits for your members.

2

Creating a Business Plan

To reach your objectives, it helps to develop a simple survey business plan that will comprise at least the following sections:

- A general description of the survey you plan to produce;
- A description of the companies you plan to include in your survey;
- An estimate of the number of companies that meet your criteria and the number that may participate in the survey;
- An outline for promoting participation in the survey;
- A plan to promote the sale of the survey;
- A description of work assignments and assigned responsibilities;
- Cost estimates for designing, producing, and distributing the survey;
- Revenues and profit you expect to achieve

When making decisions on your business plan, always look at your survey from the point of view of increasing participation and focusing on what information the survey user, members and non-members, will find valuable.

What information should a general description of our survey contain?

The information that your survey will contain will also affect the number of companies that will be attracted to participate. There are multiple areas to consider:

A description of the categories and levels of benchmark jobs you will include in the survey. Questions to answer include: Will we focus on only non-exempt jobs? Only production jobs? Will the survey include information on management jobs? To what level? And so on.

The content and organization of the information the survey will present. Questions to answer in this section relate to the kind of information you will present. For example: Will you provide data in categories determined by company employment size or industry? Will you provide data on salary range values or only on actual salaries? Selecting data categories in advance may be done on a tentative basis. Once all of the survey records are collected more appropriate data categories may be revealed.

The method of delivering the survey to the user. The questions to be answered here include: Will the survey be printed and mailed to participants and purchasers? Will it be delivered as an electronic file for printing? Will survey users be able to analyze the data? Will the survey file be in an interactive format allowing the survey user to enter search criteria when obtaining a survey report?

What kind of companies should we include in our survey?

In most cases your association's profile will define your targeted companies, either by industry, geography, or both. However, it would be wise to think beyond just your association's profile and include companies from which your members may recruit their employees.

For example, if your association comprises only credit unions, the companies you target for your survey might also include savings or commercial banks, especially if the survey will focus on jobs common to both kinds of organizations, like tellers and branch managers.

How can we estimate the number of companies that might participate in the survey?

To accomplish this, start with your own association's member list. Add to this any other companies that fit your survey's participant profile. The names of other potential survey participants may be obtained from the member lists of other associations similar to yours. Local business associations, such as chambers of commerce, or magazine subscription lists may also be available. For a fee, marketing list vendors can also provide access to potential survey participants.

Also, consider what other salary surveys are already available in your market. Covering the same ground as salary surveys currently being published in your area or industry will diminish the interest in your survey, unless you can offer different information, higher quality information, or similar information at a reduced price. The question is: What will make your survey more attractive to customers than those currently available? If all of your association members are in the same industry, you may be able to offer information on industry-specific jobs that are not available anywhere else. Or, perhaps you can generate more accurate data through a larger sample size for your region that national surveys cannot offer.

Here are a few guidelines to help you estimate how many companies will participate in your survey. If you are dealing with your association members, a participation rate of 10% to 20% would be fine. If your association is small, and the members have committed to participating in the survey in advance, your participation rates will be much higher. For non-members, a participation rate of up 3.0% to 5.0% would be excellent.

How will we promote interest in our survey?

Keep in mind that every survey purchaser will want to know two things about your survey:

- What are the types and location of companies in the survey sample?
- What benchmark jobs are represented in the survey?

If the potential purchaser of a survey does not view the participants as competitors in the labor market or does not recognize many of the survey benchmark jobs as existing in his company, then he will probably not be willing to purchase a survey.

There are many creative ways to promote interest and increase the sale of your survey. Here are a few examples:

- Telephone calls or emails to the human resources managers of targeted companies
- Ads in local business newspapers or trade journals
- Ads in the association's magazine or on-line publications
- A survey link on the association's website
- Providing complimentary copies of the past surveys at association or industry trade shows
- Press releases on the initial findings of the survey
- Announcements of the surveys availability at member meetings
- Creation of a webinar on "The Use of Salary Surveys" for members

How should we organize the work that needs to get done to finish the survey?

The survey production process will need to be managed; and, there are a number of tasks that will need to be completed to finish the process. Most likely you will want to create a project team that will manage each of the steps involved in the survey design and production process. Here is one example of how work might be organized.

Survey Team Leader

Someone will need to lead the salary survey effort. Ideally this would be a person with a background in compensation who understands salary survey methodology and use. You might consider hiring a compensation consultant to perform this role if none of your members have this kind of expertise.

Among other responsibilities, the leader's job will be to select and train team members, plan and assign work, ensure that tasks are accomplished, and make decisions about what is included and excluded from the final survey document or file.

Project Teams

Here are descriptions of teams that might be formed to complete the work required to produce and sell a salary survey. Volunteers may serve on one or more teams.

1. A team or steering committee to discuss and resolve all of the survey design issues involved in producing the final survey documents. Design issues to be resolved include:

- The selection of benchmark jobs to include in the survey
- The creation of forms to capture contact information on participants

- The composition of instructions for completing the survey
- The selection of topics related to compensation policies and practices
- The design of survey forms to collect information on compensation policies and practices
- The design of salary data collection forms
- The design and organization of data in the final salary survey output document

2. A team to compose the summary job descriptions that will be used by survey participants in their job matching efforts.

Information on benchmark job summaries can be gathered from existing surveys, member job descriptions, or interviews with members themselves. The description should be brief, but it should contain the essential functions and minimum requirements of the job so that good job matches can be made.

3. A team to check the survey forms or spreadsheets that are returned

Very often volunteers can be used in this role. If they have some experience with salary surveys, it will save time. If they have no such experience, the leader will need to provide instruction on checking survey return forms, i.e. where to look for errors, what is acceptable and what is not, etc. As mentioned above, data checking can be improved by the use of formulae in spreadsheet applications. Very often errors noted in this way can be resolved immediately. Ultimately, however, any apparent errors involving job matching or guessing will need to be resolved by contacting the survey respondent.

Volunteers may make the initial call to respondents to resolve discrepancies. However, when issues cannot be resolved the survey leader will need to make decisions on what will be accepted and what will not. Discussions with companies submitting data will clarify most situations.

4. A team to enter records into the survey database and generate the final report

Once again, a volunteer can be useful here. If paper forms are used, one or more association members with good keyboard/ computer skills may be able to handle this data entry task. In the past, survey data was often transcribed from paper forms into a computer database. More recently, the processing of survey data involves transferring data from one electronic form, e.g. Excel, into a database such as Access and then generating the final survey report.

Many software programs have powerful data transfer capabilities which can be used to your advantage. However, such a strategy requires more planning and system design up front.

Survey reports are generally produced from a database or spreadsheet program into a printed or electronic document format, such as Adobe. A volunteer member having the requisite expertise will be able to produce and create the survey file. If such talent does not exist with your organization, you will need to contract for these services with an outside consultant.

5. A team to coordinate the printing of the final survey and order fulfillment

If the survey is to be provided in a hard copy format, someone will need to arrange for the printing and binding of the survey reports. Once the computer has printed out all of the pages of the survey, these pages will need to be delivered to a printer. The number of copies you order will depend on how many copies you estimated you would need in your project plan.

The survey binding should provide ease of survey use. Spine bindings that allow the survey to lie flat are excellent.

Someone will need to respond to orders that are received for the survey. The designated person needs to be identified as the point of contact in any material used to promote the sale of the survey as the point of contact. To prepare for this role, this person will need to understand the terms of sale and the latitude, if any, that will be given with regard to them. Terms of sale include when payment is due, what form of payment is acceptable, what circumstances would support a refund, etc.

6. A team to increase sales of the survey

Very often this work can be done by volunteers who are willing to make telephone calls to prospective survey purchasers, write copy for ads, flyers, etc., or staff booths at association trade shows.

How can we estimate the cost for designing, producing, and distributing the survey?

- The primary contributors to cost to be considered here are:
    - The process for designing and producing the survey input forms and final report
    - The means by which you intend to collect survey responses
    - The cost for producing the survey report
    - The means for distributing the survey report to participants and non-participants (*See Exhibit 2: Calculating the Cost of Producing Your Survey*)

Once you have an estimate of the cost of producing your salary survey, you will be able to decide if you intend the revenue from the survey to cover all, a portion, or none of this cost. You might make the survey free to members, but offer it at a price to non-members. As stated previously, surveys are often regarded as a very valuable service by members, and, if well done, can elevate the prestige of your association.

How can we estimate the revenue and profit we can reasonably expect to generate from our survey?

To determine the revenue potential for your survey, you will need to:

1. Estimate the size of the potential market for different groups. For example, you might decide to create different price levels for each of the following:

    *   Participating association members;
    *   Non-participating association members;
    *   Participating non-members; and,
    *   Non-participating non-members.

You might also choose to offer special discounts to members of associations not your own. For example, if your association is a chapter of the Society for Human Resources Management (SHRM), you might offer your survey at a discount to the members of other SHRM chapters that are in the same geographic region as your own.

2. Determine the price you will charge for your survey for each group. The price you charge to each group will be a function of your business and profit objectives. Also, to be competitive, you may need to consider the average cost of surveys being offered for sale in your market. *(See Exhibit 3: Calculating the Price for Your Survey)*

3

Determining the Information Your Survey Will Contain

In this section, we will concentrate on what information you intend to provide to those companies that purchase your association's survey. Contacting a sample of your market, especially your members, to discuss the nature and scope of the information they would like to have is a great idea. You might want to establish a steering committee of prominent Human Resources professionals to oversee the actual design and production of the survey. It is a great way to promote involvement, gain support and establish credibility for the survey itself.

The information that your survey will contain will include all or most of the following:

- Benchmark job summaries
- Data on the components of compensation for each benchmark job organized by various categories
- Information on selected policies or practices related to compensation
- Other information that may be helpful to the survey purchaser in understanding or using the survey results

What is a benchmark job?

A benchmark job is any job that commonly exists in the companies that you expect to participate in your survey. Jobs that are unique to a particular company are not good benchmarks. One example of this would be jobs that are sometimes referred to as hybrid jobs. For instance, the payroll manager in a certain company might also be responsible for the mail room. This is not a common set of responsibilities and, therefore, may not be a good benchmark. I once worked in a company where the executive chauffeur also worked as a benefits claims clerk. Also, not a useful benchmark.

Useful benchmark jobs can exist in all industries or in only one industry. Jobs common to all industries include such jobs as payroll clerks, administrative assistants, accountants, human resources assistants, receptionists, and many others. Any of these would serve well as a benchmark job. Good benchmark jobs may exist only in certain industries, such as tellers, claims adjusters, electro-mechanical assemblers, medical claims processors, and others. It is not uncommon for a survey, even one targeted to a specific industry, to contain both specific and common benchmark jobs.

Another thing to be aware of is that benchmark jobs should, if possible, represent the entire range of job values in the market from the lowest to the highest. This will make it possible for survey purchasers to set market values for all of the levels of pay in their organizations. A cross-industry survey might include jobs from Mail Clerk up to Controller, or even higher. Even surveys that focus on a particular profession, such as electronic engineering, might include jobs from the lowest level of engineering technician, through multiple levels of engineers, to multiple levels of management in that division.

To be sure, your choice of benchmark jobs will be determined by the industry and location of the companies that comprise your membership.

Consider also, that your selection of benchmark jobs will also have an effect on the geographic scope of your survey. Labor markets expand as the level of job responsibility increases. So, for example, the competitive market for non-exempt jobs is very local. The competitive market for managers may be regional; and the market for senior executives is often considered to be national.

Which benchmark jobs should we include in our survey?

Deciding the kind of benchmark jobs that will be included in your survey is a key decision. As stated above, the decision to purchase a copy of your survey will depend, in great measure, on the benchmark jobs it contains. Always remember... Good job matching is an essential part of any good salary survey process.

If all of the companies in your organization are in the same industry, you might want to concentrate on industry-specific jobs (e.g. electro-mechanical assembler or teller). If you have multiple industries represented in your association, you will probably concentrate on cross-industry jobs (e.g. a payroll clerk or systems analyst).

How do we go about writing benchmark jobs summaries?

When writing benchmark job summaries, you should begin by

developing a list of the jobs you intend to make part of your survey. After a careful discussion to determine which jobs match the criteria described above, select the jobs that will be most valuable to your members and to other companies as well.

There are multiple sources of basic information on many benchmark jobs. These include:

- Job summaries in existing salary surveys
- Job descriptions from member companies
- Interviews with association members to provide information on job duties
- Websites like www.occupationalinfo.org

Once you have the basic information, you will probably need to edit the information to produce a good benchmark job summary for your survey. Remember, the benchmark job summary will be used by survey participants for matching to the jobs in their organizations. The goal of this exercise is to produce a summary that will be broad enough to result in as many matches as possible, and yet specific enough to represent the job accurately... a real balancing act.

What are the elements of a good benchmark job summary?

There are three elements that are contained in a good benchmark job summary. These are:

- A description of the job responsibilities
- Minimum requirements
- Comments on a good match

A Description of Job Responsibilities

In the instructions you provide to participants, you will be asking for a 75% match, meaning that the responsibilities described in the job summary represent those being performed by the employees in that job at least 75% of the time. Therefore, the summary you write should focus on the <u>primary du-</u><u>ties of the job only</u>. Usually three to five sentences will be sufficient to accomplish this.

Minimum Requirements

You will improve the quality of the matches made if you give the participant some idea of the educational level, years of experience, and any other minimum requirements for the job. Other minimum requirements would usually include: 1) Licenses or certifications; or, 2) Required skill levels, such as typing skill expressed in words per minute.

Comments on a Good Match

Very often, survey providers will provide comments in the benchmark summaries to improve the quality of the job match. Here are a few examples:

- "This position represents the first level of exempt supervision and does not include working supervisors."
- "Incumbents in this position usually report to the President or Chief Executive Officer."
- "Include only Branch Managers in branches with more than $1,000,000 in assets."

What levels or types of jobs should we include in our survey?

Of course, you should be collecting information on full-time positions. However, in our economy, the level of part-time or per diem employment has been increasing, and will probably continue to do so. Many employers have an interest in wage levels for these groups. In some industries, such as health-care, per diem workers are a vital part of the workforce and should be included.

If you decide to include part-time or per diem jobs in your

survey, you should consider reporting this information separately from the full-time wage information. Part-time wages can vary significantly from full-time wages for two reasons: 1) Higher turnover in part-time jobs can result in lower average pay levels; and, 2) Some companies have pay policies that may pay less or more for part-time employees depending on their eligibility for medical benefits and other factors.

Finally, before you proceed, you will need to develop a definition of what you mean by part-time employee. Your definition could be as broad as: "Any employee that does not have a regular, full-time schedule," or as narrow as: "Employees who work a regular, part-time schedule of at least 20 hours per week." This definition will need to be included in the instructions you prepare for completing the survey.

What information should we offer in our survey and how should it be organized?

The information you will present to those who purchase your survey and the organization of that information will be influenced by common practice, the culture of the industry you are focusing on, and the needs of your association members.

It is common practice for survey providers to include standard statistical metrics in salary surveys. These include a straight average, a weighted average, and multiple percentile values. All of these can be used by the survey purchaser to isolate and define external equity issues with regard to compensation.

In what way does the industry affect how survey data is categorized?

Besides providing the overall information about each job, surveys often categorize survey data by the factors that can have an effect on salary levels. The idea is to allow survey participants to compare themselves as closely as possible to others of their kind in the market. For example, large companies may pay differently than smaller ones. Unionized companies may have higher pay scales than non-unionized companies. You will need to look for factors that might correlate to differences in salary levels and then provide averages, etc., by these factors.

The culture of an industry may dictate what kind of information is collected and how that information will be organized and categorized. For example, in the banking industry asset size is a common metric used to categorize the size of banks and bank branches. In the hospital industry, bed size is sometimes the category of choice. Non-profit organizations are often categorized by the size of their operating budget. In some industries, cash bonuses or even stock awards may be fairly common. A salary survey in such industries would need to include information on these forms of compensation in order to present a complete compensation picture.

It is commonly accepted practice to present compensation data on executive jobs by company size, usually expressed as revenue, employment size, or assets.

Here are some examples of factors that may influence salary levels.

- Company Size (Revenue or Assets)
- Company Size (Employee Population)
- Industry (Multiple Layers)
- Union Status
- Budget Size (Non-Profit Organizations)
- Kilowatt generating capacity (Size of a power plant)
- Geographical Location (National to Local)

How will the needs of our members influence the collection and display of survey information?

Always keep in mind that the purpose of the survey is to provide your members with the information they need to make sound business decisions about how their employees are compensated. Here are a few examples of how the needs of your members may determine the information your survey will contain.

Example 1: If your members are fairly large companies with formal salary administration processes, you will probably include information on policy wages, i.e. salary range values, in your survey. Conversely, if your members are small companies with less formal salary administration processes, you may not need to include this kind of information.

Example 2: In some industries, for example the independent power generation industry, plant bonuses for non-exempt employees are fairly common. Designing a survey for companies in this industry should include data on annual cash bonuses.

Example 3: Your members may wish to see how their company pay values compare to the survey data without their values being represented in the data. While presenting a more statistically accurate picture of the market, accommodating this request would make survey report processing much more complicated and costly to produce.

Example 4: Your members may wish to see all of the detail records that were submitted for each job. This gives them a much clearer view of the survey responses and how the averages were calculated.

Which components of compensation should our survey include?

There are many forms of pay. Base pay is often the only kind of pay included in salary surveys. Yet, for certain jobs, base pay alone cannot present a complete picture. Executives and sales managers or representatives often derive significant portions of their compensation from variable pay plans, i.e.

34

commissions and bonuses. These days, many companies are experimenting with different forms of variable pay at the individual or team level for employees who traditionally have never earned variable pay. In order to present a clear picture of compensation levels, consider representing a total cash compensation value (i.e. base pay plus bonuses) in your survey.

What kind of data should we publish in our survey?

There are basically two kinds of data that result from the collection of salary survey records: Detail Records and Processed Values.

- *Detail records* are the actual responses representing wage levels and other survey topics received from survey respondents. In their presentation of the survey results, some survey providers will list all of the records received and use code numbers or letters in place of company names in order to assure confidentiality.

  Publishing all of the detail information provides the most complete view of how the processed values were calculated; and yet a word of caution here... this approach can compromise confidentiality even if code numbers or letters are used in place of company names.

- *Processed values* are the averages, medians, highs, lows, etc., for each job that are calculated based on the records provided. Processed values fall into two general categories: 1) Measures of central tendency; and, 2) Measures of distribution.

Your survey will always include processed values.

What are measures of central tendency?

The key data elements in a salary survey are the <u>measures of central tendency</u>. These measures summarize all of the data reported for a job into one or several values. Here is a description of the most commonly used measures:

- *Straight Average:* The sum of all data points reported divided by the number of data points. A straight average gives equal weight to each data point (respondent). It is a useful measure especially in comparing policy rates, i.e. salary range values, since it gives equal weight to each company's decision of what the value of the job should be.

- *Weighted Average:* The weighted average is calculated by multiplying each salary data point reported by the number of employees reported to be in the job. The resulting product values are then added together and the total is divided by the total number of employees represented in that job category. Weighted average is often preferred as a measure of central tendency for actual wage data since it will reflect the influence of large and small employers in the area which are an integral part of the local labor market.

- *Median:* The median is the value which is exactly in the middle of survey response data which have been arranged in ascending or descending order. It can also be referred to as the 50th Percentile. In an odd-numbered range of data, the median is the value in the middle. For example, in a range of seven data points, the median would be the fourth data point. In an even-numbered range of data, the median is the average of the two middle points of data. For example, in a range of eight data points, the median would be the average of the fourth and fifth data points. Median is often preferred as a measure of central tendency if there are relatively few data points reported, since the averages in such circumstances can be unduly influenced by very high or low values. In addition, median tends to be a more stable measure over time, making it more useful for long-term analyses of salary growth or decline.

Median values are most often used to set an organizations pay line, that is, its preferred position in the market. So if an organization wishes to pay the "middle" of the market, it will set its salary range midpoints to be close to the market median values for comparable jobs.

The relationship between median and weighted average values can help in interpreting survey data. Weighted averages significantly above the median (right skewed) might indicate jobs typically occupied by longer service employees. Conversely, weighted averages significantly lower than median (left skewed) could indicate jobs with high turnover.

What are measures of distribution?

Measures of distribution are indicators of how valid the measures of central tendency are. An average is more valid if the data points used to calculate it are closer to it. As data points move away from the average, the less valid the average is. Perhaps you have heard about the man standing with one foot in boiling water and one foot on a block of ice. Was he really experiencing an average temperature? The point is that extreme values represented in measures of central tendency need to be noted in order for the data to be interpreted properly. In fact, some statistical methodologies used to process survey data involve excluding extreme high or low values from the sample.

Reporting all of the detail data received in ascending or descending order will give the clearest picture of how the processed data was calculated allowing the survey purchaser to exclude data that they may view as unacceptable. As stated above, this approach may compromise confidentiality.

The more common measures of distribution are:

- *Percentiles:* Percentiles divide the range of data that has been ordered from the lowest value to the highest value, into 100 parts and report values at certain points of the range. For example, if the value of the 25th percentile for a particular job is $35,000, it would mean that 25% of the values reported for that job are equal to or below $35,000. The value at the 75th percentile would represent a value equal to or higher than the data points in the bottom 75% of the range of data reported.

Published salary surveys will usually report values at the following percentiles: 25th, 50th, and 75th.

- *Standard Deviation:* Standard deviation is a statistical calculation of the variability of data around an average. The value of one standard deviation captures 34% of all data points on either side of the average. Therefore, 68% of data points are within one standard deviation, over or under the average. The higher the value of the standard deviation, the less valid is the average in representing all of the data points recorded. For example, suppose you had an average of $50,000 and a standard deviation of $5,000. This would mean that 34% of the data points are between $45,000 and $50,000. Another 34% would lie between $50,000 and $55,000. And so, 68% of the data points that make up the average lie between $45,000 and $55,000. Now suppose a standard deviation of $1,000. That would mean that 68% of the data points that make up the average lie between $49,000 and $51,000... clearly a much closer fit.

- *Distribution Analysis:* A distribution analysis breaks up the data range into logical sub-ranges and indicates the number of values within that range. For example, the distribution for a clerical position might look like this:

  $20,000 - $25,000: 5 data points

  $25,001 - $30,000: 12 data points

  $30,001 - $35,000: 8 data points

This analysis tells the survey user how the values within the sample were distributed.

Each of these measures of data distribution will give the survey user pictures of how valid the measures of central tendency displayed in the survey are, and to what degree they can be relied on.

How should we display the information that we collect in our salary survey?

There are three basic ways to display information in a salary survey: Tables, Labeled Values, and Graphs. A good statistical package may provide you with others which may be useful.

- *Tables:* Tables are lists of data arranged in columns. Each column has a heading describing what it contains. Usually the table will be arranged in ascending or descending order by one or more of the column headings. Tables are useful for reporting all of the detail data reported for a particular job. For example, you might list Company Code in the first column, then Reported Job Titles in the second column and so forth. *(See Exhibit 4: Survey Report Form with Detailed Records)*

  Another use of tables would be to summarize survey data by the various factors such as company size, etc., as noted above. For example, you might list the Survey Job Title in the first column, and then list the salary averages for that job for each survey data category, such as Union Companies, Non-Union Companies, Large Companies, Small Companies, etc.

- *Labeled Values*: Labeled values are typically used to identify measures of central tendency or other processed data in the survey report. *(See Exhibit 4: Survey Report Form with Detailed Records)* Usually these values appear alone or at the bottom of a table of a detailed data table. Examples of labeled values would be: Average,

Weighted Average, 25th Percentile, and 50th Percentile (Median).

- *Graphs:* There are many kinds of graphs that can be used to display the results of a survey question. Here are a few:

  - *Line Graphs*: Line graphs are useful for representing changes in value over time or as related to a series of other values, e.g. Salary Increase Budgets for the past five years.

  - *Bar Graphs:* Bar graphs are useful in distribution analysis when representing the number of values in each salary category, when representing multiple salary levels of the same job family, or when representing different salary levels based on factors such as company size.

  - *Pie Charts:* Pie charts are useful in representing the pieces of the whole. For example, you could use a pie chart in representing the companies that comprise your survey sample, i.e. 25% manufacturing, 37% financial services, 18% health care, 20% other.

  - *Regression Lines:* Regression lines represent the relationship between one or more independent variables and one dependent variable. The independent variables are factors that change in value, e.g. company size, and which correlate to changes in the dependent variable, i.e. salary level. Generally regression analysis in surveys is used for executive or management positions where salaries for particular jobs tend to vary based on company revenue, asset size, or other factors. Unless you are surveying executive or management jobs, you will probably not make use of regression analysis. *(See Exhibit 5: Explanation of Regression Analysis for more information)*

In any case, displays of data should be clear and uncluttered for ease of use by the survey user.

What information should a company profile and policy questionnaire contain?

A Company Profile and Policy Questionnaire serves three purposes.

1. To describe the survey sample by industry or size in the final report;
2. To collect information that will be used to categorize the salary information provided by respondents; and
3. To collect information about related pay issues of interest to survey respondents, such as exempt overtime, vacations, and other topics noted above.

As with any form, the Company Profile and Policy Questionnaire should be clear and organized very well. (*See Exhibit 6 for an example of Company Profile and Policy Questionnaire*)

What questions on compensation policies and practices are usually included in a survey?

Salary surveys often provide information on other related topics, which are very useful to survey users. Choose which of these you want to include very carefully. They can be very time consuming to analyze and summarize in the final survey report. Here are some to consider:

- *Salary Increase and Merit Budgets*: Respondents are asked to provide information on their current and future salary increase and merit budgets. This information is usually presented as a percentage of annual payroll. For example, if a company reports that it has a 3.0% salary increase budget, it means that it has budgeted 3.0% of its annual payroll expense for salary increases. This information is useful to help companies understand how salaries are growing in the marketplace and how to estimate the salary growth opportunity that they may wish to offer to their employees for the coming year.

Companies may offer annual salary increase opportunities to employees in various forms, including: 1) Merit increases based on job performance; 2) General or Across-the-board increases by which all employees are eligible to receive the same percentage of salary increase; 3) Market adjustments which may target specific jobs for an adjustment based on market conditions and competitive activity; and, 4) Promotions. Some companies budget their merit increases or general increases as separate items from their overall salary increase budget which will also include market adjustments and promotions.

- *Salary Structure Adjustments*: Similar to salary increase budgets, respondent companies that have and use salary ranges to administer salaries are asked to report the date and actual percent of increase to the last adjustment of their salary ranges and to provide an estimate for their next planned salary range adjustment.

- *Paid Time Off Benefits*: Vacation Pay, Holidays, Paid Sick Time, Jury Duty Pay, Military Pay, and Paid Leaves of Absence.

- *Other Existing Policies Related to Compensation*: Exempt Overtime, Shift Differentials, Family Medical Leave, and Severance Pay.

- *Types of Pay Plans*: Gainsharing, Broadbanding, Skill-Based Pay, Team Incentives, Bonuses, and Recognition Plans.

- *Work/Life Balance Policies:* Telecommuting, Flexible Work Hours, Job Sharing, Four-Day Workweeks.

(See Exhibit 6: Company Profile and Policy Questionnaire for an example)

What are special reports and how might they benefit the survey purchaser?

Special reports are those that are prepared in response to a specific request. For example, a survey purchaser may ask for a survey report containing companies of only a certain size, or perhaps, the five largest companies in the survey. It is even possible for the survey purchaser to request a special report containing only data from five companies selected from the list of participants. If your survey data base is structured properly, you may be able to provide this kind of information. Companies are often willing to pay a premium for select sample cuts of data. Be careful here about confidentiality and other anti-trust issues.

What is the best way to deliver survey results to the survey purchaser?

There are three basic ways to deliver a survey:

- Hard copy or an electronic file that can be printed by the survey purchaser;
- A computer spreadsheet file; or,
- A searchable database that allows the survey user to enter search criteria and generate survey reports to their specification.

Each method has advantages and disadvantages. Paper surveys are incorruptible, easy to store and access, and very portable. A major disadvantage of providing paper surveys is that the survey user must re-enter data from the survey document into a spreadsheet application in order to complete any kind of market analysis. In addition, the cost of printing and mailing surveys can be high. Sending electronic files, i.e. Adobe, is very cost efficient; but, as with paper surveys, it is not easy to work with the survey data in completing external market analyses.

Computer spreadsheets offer the greatest flexibility to analyzing data using various sorting capabilities, pivot tables, and other spreadsheet functionalities. However, working with data in this way may require a fairly high level of expertise with computer spreadsheets.

The searchable data base offers a way to extract survey information in a less complex way focusing on the criteria that are meaningful to the survey user, such as a particular job, a targeted revenue size, or a targeted industry designation. A searchable database, however, will require a higher initial set up cost than either of the other two options.

4

Publishing a Survey with High Quality Data

There are three keys to ensuring quality salary survey data: 1) Clear instructions and data collection forms; 2) Training for participants with emphasis on careful job matching; and 3) Aggressive data scrubbing.

What topics should survey instructions cover?

When preparing survey instructions and forms use as much plain language as possible. Avoid highly technical terms or jargon. Provide definitions of terms that are used in the survey forms and instructions, especially those that might be unfamiliar to the participant. Provide examples whenever possible to illustrate an important point.

There are two kinds of instructions that ought to be provided to survey participants: 1) General Instructions; and, 2) Detailed Instructions.

1) General Instructions should include:

- Instructions on how to match jobs in the survey including encouragement to supply only high-quality data. Remember: Less good data is always better than more bad data.
- The name and phone number of a person to call with questions or for assistance.
- Clear instructions on the format of reporting the data. For example, you might want annual salaries reported for some jobs, and hourly rates used for other jobs.
- The effective date of salary levels and salary ranges that are to be reported in the survey. This is very important. It will allow the survey user to adjust salary data being used in an analysis for growth in the labor market since the survey data was collected. This process is sometimes called trending or "aging" the data.
- A clear indication of when the survey is due back.
- Blank spaces to record the name and address or email address of the person who is to receive a copy of the published survey.

(See Exhibit 7: General Instructions for Survey Participation for an example)

2) Detailed Instructions should include a description of the information that is to be provided for each blank space on the Survey Input Form. Instructions should be clear and specific, using examples if needed.

(See Exhibit 8: Detailed Instructions for a Survey Data Collection Form for an example)

What topics need to be discussed in a survey participant training session?

If you believe that people responding to your survey may not be familiar with salary surveys, you could offer a training session to review the survey instructions and forms. If participants are in the same geographic location, you might be able to host a meeting. If participants are disbursed, a teleconference or webinar might be more appropriate.

The agenda for the training session ought to include at least the following:

- **Survey Forms:** Review and discuss each of the survey form responses to ensure that they are understood by respondents.
- **Job Matching**: Job matching is the process by which the respondent compares jobs in his/her company to those in the survey in order to make a match. If not done properly, values being reported will not be accurate in relation to the job being surveyed. To be valid, the job summary provided in the survey should represent at least 75% of the duties in the job being reported. Make sure to provide examples of good and bad job matches.
- **Match Integrity:** Respondents should be required to match only one level of job in their company to a survey job. For example, let's say that the respondent's company recognizes five levels of engineer. However, the association's survey presents them with three levels for matching. It is better for the respondent to select three of the five levels of engineer in their company that match most closely the three levels represented in the survey, instead of trying to group two levels of engineer into one level of the survey.
- **Estimating:** Provide a discussion of how estimates might be used to respond to survey questions. Estimating values may be acceptable in some situations, however, it is not a good idea to guess (even educated

guesses) when providing survey responses.

How can we design clear survey data collection forms?

For an example of a Survey Data Collection Form see Exhibit 9. Many designs are possible and are dependent on the specific data you intend to collect and how it will be reported. A clear, well-organized data collection form will minimize mistakes in the final report.

- Generally, the Survey Data Collection Form will collect information about the job being surveyed and the actual salaries and incentives being paid. Here is a list of data elements you will probably want to include:
  - Job Profile:
    1. The survey title for the job and the job summary
    2. The survey job code number that has been assigned to that position
    3. The respondent company's job title and job code for the job being surveyed
    4. The FLSA status of the job: Exempt or Non-exempt
    5. Scheduled hours per normal work week
    6. Information on salary range values expressed in annual, weekly, or hourly terms
    7. Information on the union status of the position
  - Information on the eligibility of employees in the job to receive incentive pay
  - Incumbent Data for Full-Time and Part-Time Employees Reported Separately:
    1. The number of employees in the job
    2. Actual salaries being paid, i.e. average, lowest wage, highest wage, etc.
    3. Actual incentive earnings being paid
    4. Actual total cash compensation value being paid, i.e. average, lowest paid, highest paid, etc.

What is the process for scrubbing data collected from respondents?

Data scrubbing means carefully reviewing survey returns for obvious errors, e.g. transposition of numbers, high's reported as low's, etc., and for indications of poor job matching. Data scrubbing can be aided by computer edits. For example, you can sort the survey records by job code and reported values to isolate data points that look very high or very low. These may be signs of poor job matching by the respondent or simply incorrect data.

Computer edits can also aid in catching logical errors. For example, using formulas in a spreadsheet application you can test if the values recorded in the Salary Range Minimum field are lower than those recorded in the Salary Range Maximum field. A number of these logical checks are possible and should be used to make sure that all survey information is accurate and reliable.

When questionable data is discovered, the respondent ought to be contacted to discuss and resolve the problem. The survey project manager may have to make hard decisions on what will be included in the survey and what will not be included based on the facts discussed. Any data being report that does not represent the true value for the benchmark job represented in the survey should be discarded. Always remember that titles can be misleading. Actual responsibilities are what the job match should be based on.

Here are three examples of the kind of job matching questions that can arise.

Example #1: You receive a record for a Controller that looks very low relative to the salary data submitted by other companies. In a conversation with the survey participant, you find out that the person in the job has only limited supervisory responsibility over a part-time accounting clerk; and spends more than 80% of her time doing basic accounting work. This would not be a good match.

Example #2: You receive a record for a Payroll Clerk position that seems very high relative to the other records collected. In a discussion with the survey participant, you find out that the person in the job was previously the Payroll Manager who is set to retire in a few years and was demoted. The company reduced his responsibilities but kept his salary at its previous level. In this case, the match is good because the responsibilities of the job match the survey definition. However, the value being presented is for a Payroll Manager, not a Payroll Clerk and, therefore, the record should be discarded.

Example #3: You receive a record for a Purchasing Manager's job with a salary that looks too high. You contact the respondent and discover that the Purchasing Manager is also in charge of Safety and Security for the company. This is a hybrid job and the record should probably be discarded.

5

The Final Survey Output Document

What sections will the final survey output document contain?

The final survey is assembled from multiple components. Here is an outline of what those components might be, the order of their appearance, and what information each might contain.

Outside Cover Page: The survey title; The effective date of the salary data; Your association's name, address, phone number and logo.

Inside Cover Page: The survey title; The effective date of the salary data; A person to contact with questions or problems; A copyright statement reserving rights for your association.

Letter of Thanks to Participants: Include a few summarized comments on the information contained in the survey, e.g. the number of companies that participated and the number of jobs that are represented.

Table of Contents: A listing of all the components of the survey report with referenced page numbers.

A Survey Summary with the Following Sections:

1. An introduction containing:
   a. A description of the survey methodology for collecting, analyzing, and presenting salary data. A description of the criteria that were used to eliminate jobs from the survey, e.g. lack of sufficient records.
   b. A description of how the survey is organized.
   c. A description of how the survey data is organized.
   d. Definitions of how each of the processed data elements presented in the survey were calculated.
2. Key Findings of the Survey: Any noteworthy compensation trends or outcomes that would be of interest to the participant
3. A list of the participating companies by name
4. Participant Demographics: The size, industry, or location of survey participants.

A List Containing Each Benchmark Job in the Survey by Code Number, Title, and Page Number

A Summary of the Information Collected on Compensation Policies and Practices

The Body of the Report Containing the Salary Information That Was Collected for Each Benchmark Job

(Note: It is likely that for some benchmark jobs an insufficient number of records will have been collected to be able to report

results. It is a good idea to place pages for such jobs in the body of the report indicating this. This will demonstrate to the survey purchaser that information on a particular job was not omitted in error.)

A Listing of All of the Benchmark Job Summaries by Code and Title Used for Job Matching

A Summary of Simple Compensation Tools for Using Salary Survey Data

1. Conducting an external market analysis
2. Designing a salary ranges
3. The use of salary surveys in establishing salary increase budgets

A Glossary of Terms Used in the Survey Report

EXHIBIT 1

Antitrust Issues

The purpose of anti-trust laws, such as The Sherman Anti-Trust Act, is to ensure economic freedom and free and open competition in the marketplace in order to preserve our free-enterprise system. In August 1996, the Department of Justice (DOJ) and the Federal Trade Commission (FTC) issued Statements of Antitrust Enforcement Policy in Health Care. In this document, the DOJ and FTC defined Safe Harbor Guidelines which describe an "Antitrust Safety Zone: Exchanges of Price and Cost Information among Providers That Will Not Be Challenged, Absent Extraordinary Circumstances by the Agencies."

The more relevant extracts are presented below.

The agencies will not challenge, absent extraordinary circumstances, provider participation in written surveys of (a) prices for health care services, or (b) wages, salaries, and benefits of health care personnel, if the following conditions are met:

1. The survey is managed by a third party (e.g. a purchas-

er, government agency, health care consultant, academic institution, or trade association);

2. The information provided by survey participants is based on data more than 3 months old; and,

3. There are at least five providers reporting data upon which each disseminated statistic is based, no individual provider's data represents more than 25 percent on a weighted basis of that statistic, and any information disseminated is sufficiently aggregated such that it would not allow recipients to identify the prices charged or compensation paid by any particular provider.

Although directed specifically at health care organizations, these guidelines are considered applicable to all salary surveys.

EXHIBIT 2

Calculating the Cost of Producing a Survey

In order to reach your business objectives, you will need to know how much it will cost to produce a survey. Your business objectives and marketing plan will provide the information necessary. Following are some of the costs that will need to be determined.

Salary Survey Advertising
Here are some options:
- Cost of printing and mailing flyers: _____
- Cost of placing ads in local newspapers, etc.: _____
- Cost of purchasing mailing or emailing lists: _____
- Other promotional costs: _____

Total: $_____ (A)

Data Entry

If you intend to produce a printed or printable survey, the survey data you collect will need to be entered into a computer database or spreadsheet so that data can be checked and the final survey can be generated. If you have no members who can accomplish this, you may have to look for an outside service.

- Hours of data entry needed to input survey returns: (B)   _____
- Rate per hour for data entry services: (C)   _____
- Cost of Data Entry: (B x C):

Total: $_____ (D)

Cost of Printing, Binding, and Mailing *(if producing a printed survey)*

Printers will usually quote a price per hundred. Order as many copies of the survey as you need based on your estimate of purchasers. You will need to decide how you want your survey bound. Prices will vary from simple stapling to more costly kinds of binders. The best binders are those that will allow the survey to lie flat.

Number of members in your organization: _____

Number of companies in your market area: _____

Estimated number of copies for members: (E)   _____

Estimated number of copies for non-members: (F)   _____

Estimated number of copies to print: (E + F)

_____ (G)

Cost of printing and binding per survey (H)

_____

Cost of postage per survey (I)

_____

Total cost per survey (H) + (I)

$_____ (J)

Cost for printing and mailing survey (G + J)

$_____ (K)

Compute the Total Cost of Producing the Survey by Calculating the Sum of All the "Total" Lines (A, D, and K) in this Section.

$_____ (X)

EXHIBIT 3

Calculating the Price for a Survey

To determine the price you will charge a copy of your survey you need to focus on your profit objectives, the cost of producing the survey, and the percentage of revenue you expect to get from each purchasing group.

You could charge every purchaser the same price; but, you will probably want to differentiate the pricing for different purchasing groups. For example, you may want to offer the survey free of charge to participating members, but charge a price to members that did not participate. Also, you may want to charge non-members more than members.

Here is an outline you can use to calculate the price you might charge to each group and still achieve your profit objectives:

Total Cost of Producing Survey: (X)

Profit Objective in Dollars: (Y)

Total Target Revenue: (X + Y)

Steps:

1. Estimate the copies you think you can sell to each group
2. Enter the percent of the total target revenue goal you expect to receive from each group
3. Calculate the amount of revenue to be received from each group
4. Divide the revenue by the number of copies you believe will be sold to each group

Here is an example using $10,000 as target revenue:

	(1) Estimate of Copies To Be Sold	*(2)* Percent of Revenue Goal	*(3)* Revenue Goal: $10,000	*(4)* **Price Per Copy**
Group				
Participating members	50	10.0%	$1,000	**$20**
Non-participating members	25	20.0%	$2,000	**$80**
Participating non-members	30	35.0%	$3,500	**$117**
Non-participating non-members	15	35.0%	$3,500	**$233**
Totals:	120	100.0%	$10,000	

The amounts for non-members may be adjusted higher to promote membership, if this is also a goal of your association.

EXHIBIT 4

Survey Report with Detail Records

Job Title: Accountant   *Job Code:* P-26

Job Description:

Prepares income, balance sheet and other financial statements; analyzes financial reports and records; reviews and verifies the accuracy of journal vouchers and accounting classifications; develops improvements to existing accounting methods and procedures; and performs special analyses, i.e. cost cutting programs. Bachelor's degree in accounting or equivalent experience. Minimum three years experience.

Detail Data
Section ($000)

Total Job Population	77										Job Code:	P-26	
Co	Job	Ex/	Hrs/	No. In	Actual Salaries			Salary Ranges			Bonus		
Code	Title	NE	Wk	Pos	Avg	Low	High	Min	Mid	Max	Avg	Low	High
178	Staff Accountant	EX	40.0	3	29.0	24.1	33.2	21.2	36.5	31.8			
225	Accountant	EX	35.5	1	23.0	23.0	23.0	22.1	27.6	33.1			
247	Cost Accountant	EX	40.0	4	33.8	31.5	36.0	24.4	30.5	36.6			
288	Accountant	EX	35.0	22	34.3	23.6	25.9	25.9	32.4	38.9			
311	Staff Accountant	EX	37.5	1	37.2	37.2	37.2	26.6	33.2	39.8			
333	Staff Accountant	EX	35.0	4	43.1	39.5	46.6	28.4	35.5	42.6			
362	Accountant	EX	40.0	3	41.0	38.2	43.0	28.7	35.9	43.1			
213	Financial Analyst	EX	37.5	7	36.5	30.4	45.1	30.2	37.8	45.4			
344	Cost Accountant	EX	40.0	1	37.0	37.0	37.0	30.4	38.0	45.6			
241	Cost Accountant	EX	40.0	11	41.5	34.0	50.1	25.9	32.4	38.9	0.7	0.4	1.3
155	Int. Accountant	EX	40.0	15	29.9	23.0	45.0	22.2	27.7	33.2	1.5	1.0	2.2
297	Accountant	EX	37.5	5	35.3	32.0	40.6	27.0	33.8	40.6	2.1	1.6	2.8

Processed Data
Section ($000)

Average:			38.2		35.1	31.1	38.6	26.1	33.4	39.1	1.4	1.0	2.1
Weighted Average:			37.8		35.1	28.3	38.6	25.6	32.4	38.5	1.3	0.9	2.0
Median:			38.8		35.9	31.8	38.9	26.3	33.5	39.4	1.5	1.0	2.2

66

EXHIBIT 5

Explanation of Regression Analysis

Regression analysis is a statistical process which calculates the points on a line which have the least variation or distance from the points in a range of data. This "regression line" represents the closest relationship between one or more independent variables (e.g. company revenues) and a dependent variable (e.g. base salary). In other words, in this example, the regression line will represent the differences in base salary paid by companies of different revenue sizes.

The regression line is the visual representation of the "regression formula." Once you have the regression formula you can insert any value for the independent variable (e.g. company revenue), and calculate a value for the dependent variable (e.g. base salary).

However, not all regression formulas will produce equally valid results. The farther away the data points are from the points on the regression line, the less valid is the regression formula in its ability to calculate the value of the dependent variable. The strength of the relationship between the data points and the regression formula is called the correlation factor (r^2). If all the data points in a given sample were plotted exactly on a regression line the correlation factor would be "1", representing the strongest possible relationship between one variable and the other. If there were no relationship between the two variables, the correlation factor would be "0" and the line would be horizontal to the "x" axis. Here is an example of a regression analysis.

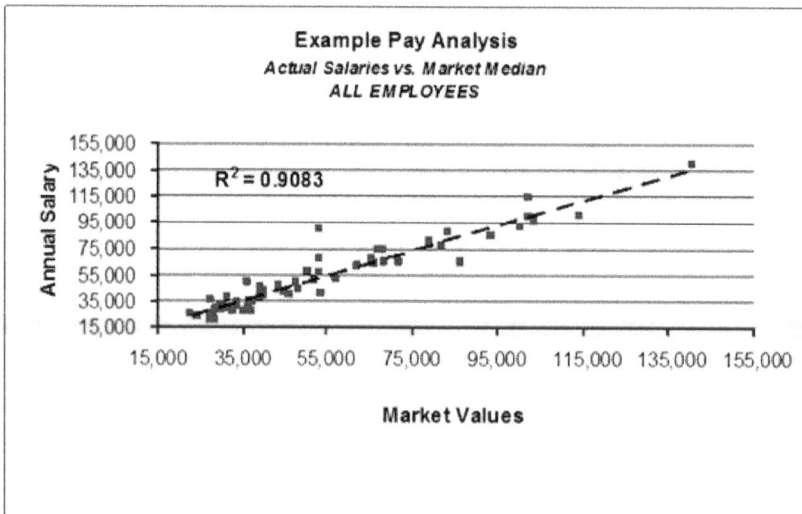

Example Pay Analysis
Actual Salaries vs. Market Median
ALL EMPLOYEES

$R^2 = 0.9083$

Annual Salary (y-axis): 15,000 / 35,000 / 55,000 / 75,000 / 95,000 / 115,000 / 135,000 / 155,000

Market Values (x-axis): 15,000 / 35,000 / 55,000 / 75,000 / 95,000 / 115,000 / 135,000 / 155,000

In this example, there is a high correlation of 0.9083 (r^2) between the market values ("x" axis) and the salaries being paid to the employees of this company ("y" axis). As you can see, most of the plotted salaries of employees are very close to the dotted regression line. Based on this analysis it appears that this company is doing a very good job of paying close to market rates.

There can also be a negative relationship between two variables, where the line slopes down from left to right. This would indicate a situation in which every increase in the value of "x" produces a decrease in the value of "y." The highest correlation factor in this case is "-1."

Generally, regression formulas are used for salary surveys involving executive positions. Since most computer spreadsheet programs have a regression analysis function built in, you will probably never have to calculate one manually. After you enter a set of values into the computer, the program will compute the regression formula, the correlation factor, as well as other statistical outcomes, such as standard error. Usually the computer will also have a function to graph the regression line if you wish to do so.

Since regression analysis often involves comparing very large values like company revenues with much smaller values, such as base salaries, surveys often use logarithmic scales and values to express the relationship. For example, the typical regression formula in an executive compensation survey might look something like this:

Log Y (Salary) = M (Slope) x Log X (Sales Revenue) + B (Y Intercept)

Here is an example:

An executive salary survey has given you the following regression equation for the base salary of a Vice President of Marketing position.

Log Y = .084 (Log X) + 1.671

Your company has sales revenue of $765 million. You need to calculate the base salary that would be paid in other companies of your size.

Divide $765,000,000 by 1,000,000 to reduce it to a 3 digit number... $765

Then...

Log (Salary) = .084 (Log 765) + 1.671

The log of 765 is 2.8837. Substituting in the formula, we have:

Log (Salary) = .084 (2.8837) + 1.671

Log (Salary) = .24223 + 1.671

Log (Salary) = 1.9132

Using a logarithm table, you can take the antilog of this number to find the salary value.

Antilog of 1.9132 = 81.9

The regression formula in this survey is indicating a salary of $81,900 for a company with sales revenue of $765,000,000.

Standard Error:

In addition to predicting a salary level given an independent variable such as revenue, regression analysis will provide information about how much variation there is around the regression line. This is called the standard error of estimate which is expressed as a percentage. If you increase any salary value derived from the regression formula by the standard error percentage, you will arrive at a value which is equal to or greater than 34% of the data points which are above the regression line. If you decrease a salary value by one standard error percentage, you will have calculated a value which is equal to or lower than 34% of all the data points that are below the regression line. Approximately 68% of the data points in the range will be within one standard error, with 34% above the regression line and 34% below the line.

This kind of information is useful in defining the salary range for a given position. Sometimes, companies will calculate the 25th and 75th percentiles and use these values as the minimum and maximum for salary ranges. To accomplish this, you can multiply the standard error percentage by a factor of 0.675.

In the example above, we calculated a salary of $81,900 from the regression formula we were given. If the formula had given us a standard error of, say, 0.20, we could have calculated the 75th percentile as follows:

$$75^{th} \text{ Percentile} = \$89,100 * 1 + (.20*.675)$$
$$= \$89,100 * 1 + (0.135)$$
$$= \$89,100 * 1.135$$
$$= \mathbf{\$101,129}$$

$$25^{th} \text{ Percentile} = \$89,100 / 1 + (.20*.675)$$
$$= \$89,100 / 1 + (0.135)$$
$$= \$89,100 / 1.135$$
$$= \mathbf{\$72,158}$$

EXHIBIT 6

Company Profile and Policy Questionnaire

A. *Type of Business:*

( ) Manufacturing   ( ) Retail Trade
( ) Financial Services   ( ) Computer Technology
( ) Health Care   ( ) Travel/Leisure
( ) Other

B. *Work Force Analysis:*

Total # of Employees _____

# of Employees at Location Being Surveyed _____

Percent Exempt:	_____%	Percent Non-Exempt:	_____%
Percent Union:	_____%	Percent Non-Union:	_____%

C. Regularly Scheduled Work Week for Full-Time Employees:

Exempt:	_____	Hrs/Wk
Non-Exempt:	_____	Hrs/Wk
Production/ Maintenance:	_____	Hrs/Wk

D. Salary Increase Guidelines:

Please indicate how much your company has allocated for salary increases in the current year and for the next year.

Group	Current Year	Next Year
Management	_____%	_____%
Exempt	_____%	_____%
Non-Exempt	_____%	_____%

E. Salary Structure Adjustment Guidelines:

Please indicate the percentage of increase that will be applied to your salary ranges in the current year and for the next year.

Group	Current Year	Next Year
Management	_____%	_____%
Exempt	_____%	_____%
Non-Exempt	_____%	_____%

F. Alternate Forms of Base Pay:

Are you now using or do you plan to use in the near future?

	Using	Plan to Use
Broadbanding	_____	_____
Skill-Based Pay	_____	_____

Competency Pay	_____	_____
Multi-Rater (360°) Appraisal	_____	_____

G. *Alternate Forms of Variable Pay:*

Are you now using or do you plan to use in the near future?

	Using	Plan to Use
Spot Bonuses	_____	_____
Team Based Incentives	_____	_____
Gainsharing	_____	_____
Productivity Bonuses	_____	_____
Cash Merit Bonuses (e.g., Lump Sum)	_____	_____
Profit Sharing	_____	_____

H. *Work/Life Balance Programs:*

Are you now using or do you plan to use in the near future?

	Using	Plan to Use
Telecommuting	_____	_____
Flexible Work Hours	_____	_____
Job Sharing	_____	_____
Four-Day Work-week	_____	_____
Cash Merit Bonuses (e.g., Lump Sum)	_____	_____
Profit Sharing	_____	_____

EXHIBIT 7

General Instructions for Salary Survey Participation

A survey is only as good as the data provided by participants. It is essential that you provide good quality data
for your own benefit as well as that of others. Here are
some guidelines that might help:

- *When matching your jobs to jobs defined in the
  survey, look for at least an 75% match,* meaning
  that the tasks described in the survey should represent
  those performed by the employees in your company at
  least 80% of the time. Don't force a match. It is better to submit less good data than more bad data. You
  might consider involving department managers in the
  matching process if you are unsure of the job's content.

- *It is better not to guess at a value.* Good estimates
  can be helpful in a survey; and, of course, actual data
  is the most desirable to report whenever possible. But

guessing should be avoided.

- *Call when you have questions.* Sometimes your company's approach to a certain pay component or policy may not fit the survey's outline. Or you may have a question about the meaning of a term. Calling the survey contact can help to clarify these situations.

Please report the actual salaries and range values for **exempt** employees in annual salary terms, e.g. $50,000. Report the actual wages and salary ranges for **non-exempt** employees in hourly terms, e.g. $11.25.

Survey returns are due back on _____. Salary values reported should be those effective on _____.

<u>All survey information collected will be kept strictly confidential.</u>

Please return your survey to:

> **Name of Survey Collector**
> **Company**
> **Address**
> **City, State, ZIP**
> **Phone:**

For questions, please contact _____ at (XXX) XXX-XXXX or email at _____@ _____.

EXHIBIT 8

Detailed Instructions for Survey Data Collection Form

Job Profile

- **Respondent Company's Job Title:** Record your company's title for the survey job being reported. If you have more than one title for the job, report the one closest to the survey title.

- **Respondent Company's Job Code:** Record your company's code for this job, if available.

- **FLSA Status:** Select Exempt or Non-exempt. Non-exempt jobs are those that require the payment of overtime for more than 40 hours in a week. Exempt jobs do not require the payment of overtime. Exemptions include supervisory, professional, administrative, and outside sales personnel.

- **Regular Hrs/Wk:** Record the normally scheduled hours per week for the position being reported.

- **Salary Range Values:** Record the minimum value, mid-value, and maximum value of the salary range for the position being reported (in annual, weekly, or hourly terms). If your company's salary ranges do not contain one of these values, write "N/A." If your company does not use salary ranges, please leave these spaces blank.

- **Is this position variable pay eligible?** Record here whether employees in the job being reported are eligible to receive any job related incentive payments (e.g., productivity bonuses, team incentives, sales incentives, etc.).

  If yes: Indicate whether the incentive is...

  - **Discretionary**, i.e. paid upon management's decision to pay an incentive, e.g. management bonuses; or
  - **Non-discretionary,** i.e. paid based upon a predetermined formula, e.g. sales incentives. Non-discretionary incentives are usually considered part of regular wages.

  Description: Describe the type of variable pay for which the position is eligible, e.g. profit sharing, sales incentives, management bonus, etc.

Incumbent Data

- **Number of Incumbents:** Indicate the number of employees, full- and part- time, that perform the job being reported.

- **Average Base Annual/Hourly Rate:** Record the current annual or hourly rate of base pay being received by incumbents.

- **Highest Base Annual/Hourly Rate:** Record the highest rate currently being paid to an employee.

- **Lowest Base Annual/Hourly Rate:** Record the lowest rate currently being paid to an employee.

- **Average Incentive Earnings per Hour/Year:** Include here the actual amount of incentive earnings paid to full-time employees in this job.

- **Average Total Earnings per Hour/Year:** Include here the actual earnings of employees including all forms of pay. A payroll file of W-2 earnings may be helpful here.

- **Do actual earnings include:** Overtime? Incentive Pay? Indicate and describe what other earnings are in the average reported.

EXHIBIT 9

Survey Data Collection Form

Job Title: Data Entry Operator   ***Job Code:*** C-17

Job Description:
Operates an electronic keyboard to input data to computer systems. May be responsible for verifying input and communicating with user areas.

Position Profile

Respondent Company's Job
Title:_____

Job Code:_____

FLSA Status: Exempt_____ Non-Exempt_____

Regular Hrs/Wk: _____

Salary Range:
Minimum $_____
Midpoint $_____
Maximum $_____

Is this position covered by a union contract?
Yes_____ No_____

Is this position variable pay eligible?
Yes_____ No_____

If yes, is incentive:
Discretionary?_____
Non-Discretionary?_____

Description:_____

Incumbent Data

Full-Time Employees
Number of Incumbents: _____
Average Base Hourly Rate: $_____
Highest Base Hourly Rate: $_____
Lowest Base Hourly Rate: $_____

Actual Incentive Earnings:
Average: $_____
Low: $_____
High: $_____
Average Total Earnings/Hour: $_____

Part-Time Employees
Number of Incumbents: _____
Average Base Hourly Rate: $_____
Highest Base Hourly Rate: $_____
Lowest Base Hourly Rate: $_____

Average Actual Earnings/Hour: $_____

EXHIBIT 10

Glossary

Annual Incentive Earnings	Cash compensation paid to an employee in addition to the employee's regular base salary over the prior 12-month period. Annual incentive earnings do not include overtime earnings or shift differentials.
Average	The sum of a group of values divided by the number of values in the group.
Benchmark Jobs	Jobs that typically exist in other companies for which survey data can be collected.
Bonus/Non-Discretionary	A cash award paid to an employee, usually on an annual basis, for performance against pre-determined goals and objectives. Bonuses may be based on individual performance, department performance, or company performance.

Bonus /Discretionary	A cash award paid to an employee, usually on an annual basis, at the discretion of management.
Broadbanding	The use of very wide salary ranges which comprise the values of two or three traditional salary ranges. Broadbanding is often employed as a strategy to simplify the salary administrative process and to allow for greater flexibility in work assignments and employee development.
Data Scrubbing	The process by which salary survey records are reviewed and adjusted to ensure high quality.
Detail Records	The actual records submitted to the survey producer from survey participants.
Distribution Analysis	An analysis that shows how the values of a given data set are distributed using a pre-determined set of ranges or values.
Exempt Overtime	A compensation practice of paying overtime to employees who meet one of the exemptions provided under the Fair Labor Standards Act.
External Equity	The relationship of a company's pay for various jobs to comparable jobs in the external market.
Family Medical Leave Act	A Federal law that requires companies to provide unpaid leave to employee for reasons related to illness and dependent care.
Flexible Work Hours	An arrangement within some companies that allows employees to vary the start-time and end-time of their work day within established parameters.

FLSA	The Fair Labor Standards Act which regulates the payment of minimum wages and overtime premiums to employees.
Four-Day Workweeks	An arrangement by some companies that extends the hours of the normal work day, which results in fewer days being worked within a one week or two week cycle.
Gainsharing	An incentive plan based on sharing a portion of reduced costs, e.g. labor costs or material costs, with employees.
Hybrid Jobs	Jobs that combine responsibilities of more than one traditional job. For example, a payroll manager who also has responsibility for purchasing.
Input Forms	Survey input forms are those provided to survey participants to record and send in their salary information.
Job Matching	Job matching is the process by which the respondent compares jobs in his/her company to those in the survey in order to make a match. If not done properly, values being reported will not be accurate in relation to the job being surveyed. To be valid, the job summary provided in the survey should represent at least 75% of the duties in the job being reported.
Job Sharing	A practice under which two part-time employees share the responsibilities of one full-time position.
Jury Duty Pay	Pay received by employees for serving on juries.

Match Integrity	Respondents should be required to match only one level of job in their company to a survey job. For example, let's say that the respondent's company recognizes five levels of engineer. However, the association's survey presents them with three levels for matching. It is better to select three of the five levels of engineer in your company that match most closely the three levels represented in the survey, instead of trying to group two levels of engineer into one level of the survey.
Measures of Central Tendency	A value that summarizes and represents the other values in a data set.
Measures Of Distribution	Statistical values that display the amount of variation in the values around an average or other measure of central tendency.
Median	The value of the data point that is exactly in the middle of an ordered set of values. The median is the same as the 50th Percentile. (*See percentiles below*)
Non-Participating Members	Members of your association that would like to purchase a salary survey, but who have not participated in the survey.
Non-Participating Non-Members	Organizations that are not members of your association that would like to purchase a salary survey, but who have not participated in the survey.

Paid Sick Time	A benefit offered by many organizations that provides pay for days that the employees is unable to work due to illness.
Participating Members	Members of your association that would like to purchase a salary survey, and who have participated in the survey.
Participating Non-Members	Organizations that are not members of your association that would like to purchase a salary survey, and who have participated in the survey.
Percentiles	Any of the 100 equal parts into which the range of the values of a set of data can be divided in order to show the distribution of those values. The percentile of a given value is determined by the percentage of the values that are equal to or less than that value. For example, a test score that is at the 95th percentile is equal to or greater than 95% of all test scores.
Processed Values	The values represented in salary surveys that are arrived at by calculations done on the records in the survey database.
Recognition Plans	Plans that provide cash or non-cash awards to employees who are chosen for demonstrating excellent work behaviors.

Salary Increase And Merit Budgets	A salary increase budget is the amount of money, expressed as a percent of annual payroll, that a company intends to spend on salary increases for the coming year. The merit budget is that component of the salary budget, which will be used to recognize individual performance as determined by management.
Salary Ranges	A device used to administer salary levels and salary growth over time, usually expressed in minimum and maximum values, and often containing midpoints or other intra-range values.
Salary Structure Adjustments	Adjustments, usually made on an annual basis, to salary ranges, usually expressed in percentage terms, to account for growth in the labor market.
Severance Pay	An amount of money offered to employees for involuntary losses of a job due to layoffs, etc. Severance pay is often calculated based on the employee's length of service with the company.
Shift Differentials	Additional pay offered to employees who work hours that are scheduled outside of the traditional work day.
Skill-Based Pay	A program that increases an employee's base pay in relationship to the employee's acquisition of new skills.
Standard Deviation	A measure of dispersion in a frequency distribution, equal to the square root of the mean of the squares of the deviations from the arithmetic mean of the distribution.

Survey Purchaser	A company that purchases a salary survey. Survey purchasers may be participants or non-participants.
Team Incentives	Incentive paid to employees based on the performance metrics measured at the team level. Some team incentives will also have an individual performance component.
Telecommuting	A work arrangement that allows the employee to work from a remote location, usually from home.
Vacation Pay	A paid time off benefit offered by most organizations to their employees. The benefit often increases with years of service.
Weighted Average	An average in which each salary to be averaged is assigned a weight which comprises the number of employees being paid at that salary. These weightings determine the relative importance of each quantity on the average. Weightings are the equivalent of having that number of employees at the same salary accounted for in the average.

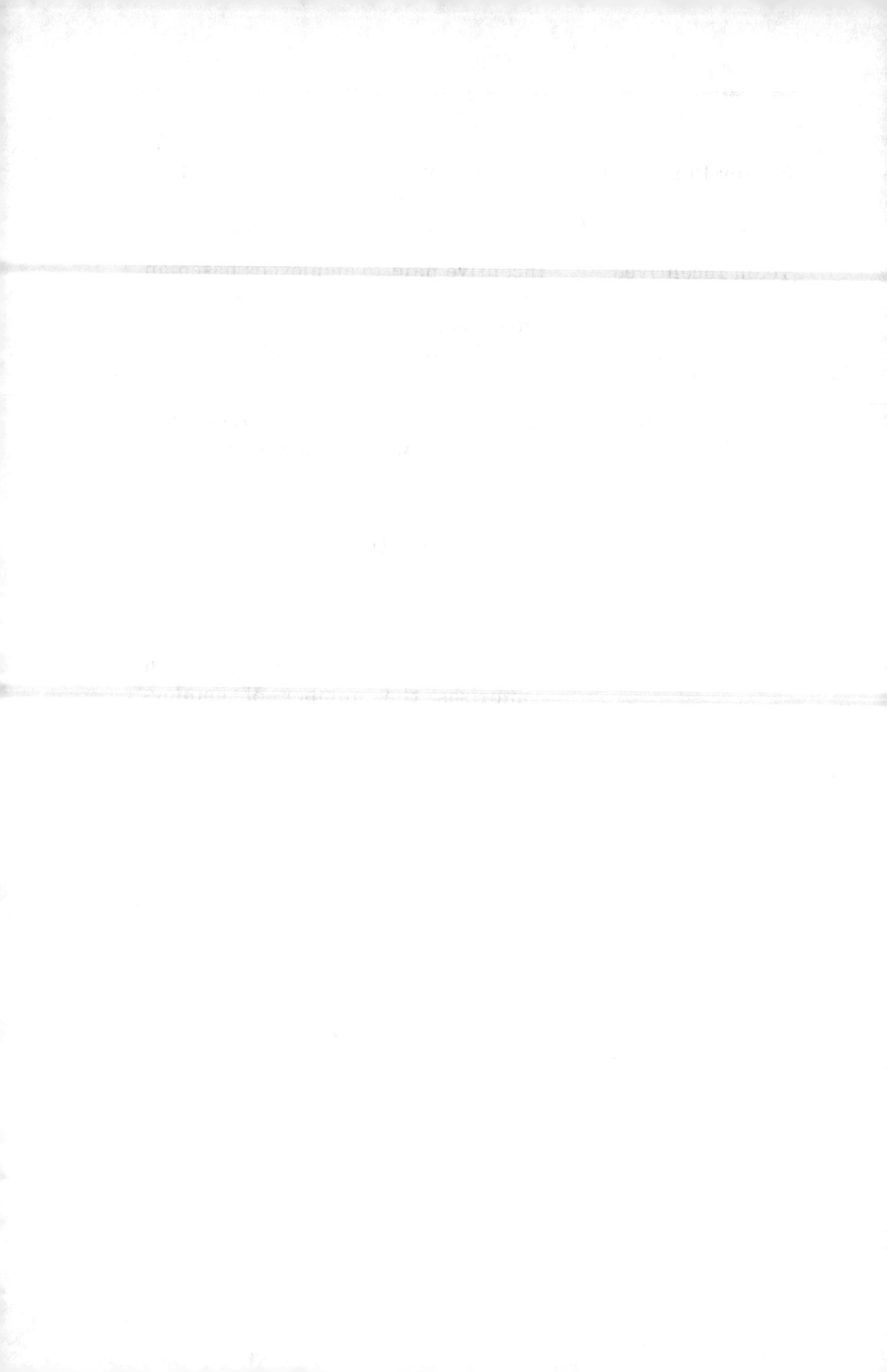

EXHIBIT 11

Questions and Answers

- **How much time should we allow for respondents to send in their survey returns?**
  The time you allow participants to respond to your survey will depend on the number of benchmark jobs in the survey and the amount of information you are asking for. However 30 to 60 days would not be uncommon.

  Also, you will need to anticipate your response it participants call and ask for more time. This is a judgment call. If multiple participants are asking for more time, or if the participant asking is a key player in the market place, then being flexible might be the best option.

- **Suppose a respondent sends in only a few survey records just to get a free survey. Should we consider them a valid participant?**
  It is sometimes wise to set a minimum number of job matches for a survey return to be useful. If you choose this option, be sure to make it explicit in the survey instructions. The limit will depend on the number of benchmark jobs in the survey. Such a limitation will probably have the effect of eliminating small companies.

- **Should we conduct a debriefing meeting after the survey has been completed?**
  De-briefing after the survey is completed is a good idea. Topics to cover include a review of jobs that did not survey well, requests for additional jobs received from participants, and suggestions from participants for making the survey easier to deal with. Also reviewing your success in selling the survey might uncover areas of additional opportunities.

- **What is the best way to promote the sale of our survey?**
  One of the best ways to promote the sale of a survey is through the regular communications channels you have established with your members, such as email blasts or newsletters. One word of advice... It may take a while to establish your survey in the market, so be patient.

- **How much are companies usually willing to pay for a survey?**
  Companies will spend $2,000 to $3,000 for surveys published by the large consulting firms. However, small regional or association surveys usually are priced from around $100 to $500. Survey participants, those who contribute data, are given deep discounts of 50% or more.

- **When is the best time of year to publish a salary survey?**
  Many companies are looking for salary information when they begin preparing their budgets for the coming year, i.e. the end of the third calendar quarter or the beginning of the fourth.

- **Suppose we find out that an error was made in one of the survey calculations. What should we do?**
  Prepare and send out a communication to the survey purchasers as soon as possible with the corrected information.

About DataMotion Publishing

We Turn Experts into Authors

DataMotion Publishing was originally established to provide books, training materials and other published periodicals to Employment Practices Advisors, Inc., a human resources consulting firm.

Now a full service publishing business, DataMotion provides publishing and related support services to subject matter experts ranging from how-to guides, training materials and practitioners resources focusing on the human resources, legal and general business areas.

Services include:
- Manuscript Services
- Interior Book Design Services
- Cover Design
- Marketing and Promotion Services
- Book Website Development and SEO
- Registration Services

Our team of experts includes not only publishing and related professionals but also experienced writers and experts in the human resources, legal and business arenas.

www.datamotionpublishing.com
info@datamotionpublishing.com